THE
Archive Photographs
SERIES

GOLDTHORPE
THURNSCOE AND
BOLTON-UPON-DEARNE

Some of the Goldthorpe Colliery miners who set a new area production record in 1986. (Courtesy of the *South Yorkshire Times*).

THE
Archive Photographs
SERIES

GOLDTHORPE THURNSCOE AND BOLTON-UPON-DEARNE

Compiled by
Dearne Local History Group
and Matthew Young

CHALFORD

First published 1996
Copyright © Dearne Local History Group and Matthew Young, 1996

The Chalford Publishing Company
St Mary's Mill, Chalford,
Stroud, Gloucestershire, GL6 8NX

ISBN 0 7524 0361 3

Typesetting and origination by
The Chalford Publishing Company
Printed in Great Britain by
Redwood Books, Trowbridge

The Dearne Local History Group would like to dedicate this book to Miss Annie Senior (left) and the late Betty Hutson (right).

Contents

Acknowledgements

My thanks must go to everyone who loaned pictures or added valuable information and help in compiling this edition.

Louise Whitworth and Gillian Nixon at the Barnsley Archive Service are always friendly, helpful, extremely professional (and not a little mad); Dearne Local History Group including Walter Norris, Hazel Follows, John Malpass, John Noble, John Jenkins, Gordon Devonport, Eric Venables, Alice Sanderson, Jean Kiely, Frieda Venables, Ron Crossland. The Group does sterling and important work in researching and writing about the history of the area. Both the Archive Service and History Group can provide a secure home for any local people wishing to safeguard their old pictures and ephemera for future generations. Mr J. Kempson for the use of his exhibition pictures; The *South Yorkshire Times* for permission to use some of their pictures of local events; Martin Kerslake for his computer advice; Scott Lambert for suggesting a book on the Dearne villages would be a worthwhile venture; Ashley Owers – because I like her; Peter Tuffrey for his excellent photographs.

Any errors, omissions or inaccuracies are entirely the fault of the author. However I would appreciate and welcome any further information (or critical assessment) concerning the pictures and text presented here.

High Street, Bolton from a picture by E.L. Scrivens of 1900.

Introduction

Within contemporary society there is a constant need to justify history as a useful and marketable concern. It has often been regarded with disdain by politicians: it does not produce wealth and it cannot employ people, therefore it has little place in the modern world than as luxury for academic minds; for the layman, history has often been a long series of facts moulded into a bland whole. This insidious atmosphere dictates to the next generation that the past is unimportant, the future everything. History is vital – attempting to justify it is akin to justifying one's own existence. All of modern society is built upon the lessons learnt from the past. As George Santayana stated in *The Life of Reason*: 'Those who ignore history are destined to relive it'. The pictures presented here do not simply let us wallow in nostaglia but remind us that the past was real – just like now. The modern urban area of the Dearne was carved out over one hundred years ago by the ancestors of contemporary residents and these images are a testament to the foundation and growth of that community. Each picture rewards the receptive eye: the bustling, congested Doncaster Road at the turn of the century; boys in knee-length shorts, girls in pinafores, men in caps; old back to back streets long since demolished; parades, carnivals, jubilees and even weddings.

The Dearne area is fortunate in having a comprehensive pictorial record of over a century of change. In no small part this has been due to the tireless work of Dearne Local History Group in collecting and collating pictures from a variety of sources. Everyone and anyone who has memories of old Dearne has been chased up and interviewed. The Dearne area now has a picture archive and a fascinating recorded history of which to be proud. The oral memories books produced by the group almost every year helped to provide much of the information for each picture. My thanks must go to all the members who allowed me to impose upon their time without a grumble.

An extensive archive is also kept by the Barnsley Archive Service. Anyone interested in the history of the Dearne or other areas within the Metropolitan area will enjoy a browse through the documents, pictures and other treasures stored at the Central Library. Many thanks must go to all staff at the Library for there kindness and patience.

Over the last few years the area has seen the pits close, businesses shut and much of the precious income generated seep slowly away. However recent investment in the Fields End project and industrial regeneration around the region may begin to breath new life into the Dearne. The sense of community and shared experience that resides throughout is one worth fighting for. I very much hope that these pictures will demonstrate what has been achieved in the past and what the people are capable of in the future.

Matthew Young,
Sheffield, 1996

A very rare photograph of Hickleton and Thurnscoe station c. 1905.

One
Goldthorpe

The Doncaster to Barnsley Road at Goldthorpe c. 1900. This ancient packhorse route linked the salt mines and local industries of Cheshire with Doncaster and the east coast ports. The track was commercialised by a Turnpike Act of 1740. The provisions of a Turnpike Act allowed the construction or maintenance of a road by the payment of tolls – a form of road building that may well be coming back into fashion. The tollhouse for the area was situated just to the east of Pickhills Avenue.

A view down Doncaster Road c. 1910. The buildings on the right, which today house Fennings DIY and Hollywoods Clothing, were once part of a single frontage owned by John Bakewell; a superstore of its time Bakewell's sold everything from beef to buckets. In May 1915, after the sinking of the Cunard Liner *Lusitania* anti-German feeling was running high throughout the country. Schonut's butchers in Goldthorpe (the Schonut's were of German extraction) was the target of an arson attempt. Local gossip insisted that Mr Schonut had been passing secret messages back to Germany by hiding them in hams. The following night rumours had spread that the Bakewell family were related to the Schonut's and an angry crowd gathered outside the store. John Bakewell and his sons armed themselves with revolvers and during the ensuing riot and looting six men were shot. One of the men, Jack Eades, was to die of his wounds several days later. Further along on the left are the 'Old Brick Row' of shops and houses which were demolished in 1959 to make way for Arndale House shops which occupy the site today.

Doncaster Road at the junction with the High Street, Goldthorpe c. 1910. It is at this point that Doncaster Road becomes retitled Barnsley Road.

The corner of Doncaster Road and High Street c. 1900. The building to the left is the Police Station and the shops which today occupy the sites further along the Barnsley Road have yet to be built.

A busy scene at Doncaster Road as tram passengers disembark c. 1925.

Doncaster Road, Goldthorpe c. 1920. The Empire on the left was owned by the Simkins family and managed by Mr and Mrs Webb; today it houses Kwik Save and Scott's Jewellers.

The Church of St John the Evangelist at Goldthorpe was designed and built in the early twentieth century from a gift from the Earl of Halifax. It's most notable features include an Italian concrete style bell tower and ornately carved pulpit.

Opposite: A view down Furlong Road on the border of Goldthorpe and Bolton c. 1920. These row of houses had the distinctive nickname of 'Packey's Puzzle'. When the debt collector (the packet man) began his weary task at the bottom of the road, a series of knocks upon the walls of each house would follow, warning neighbours of his approach. This would allow sufficient time for individuals or whole families to either leave or hide and therefore successfully thwart any attempts to collect payments for goods bought the previous week. The packet man would then be left with the 'puzzling' question of why tenants were never at home on collection day.

The Medical Officer of Health was also less than complementary about the residents of Packey's Puzzle, as quoted in John Threkeld's *Pits 2* : 'In many places about Main Street and Packey's Puzzle tenants of the houses take no pride whatever in keeping their yards clean and tidy but throw their household rubbish about the yards'. However this somewhat indignant official later stated he was 'pleased to report that fewer pigs are being kept in the back yards' .

Regulars outside the Goldthorpe Hotel c. 1910. The ornate surround to the doorway has since been removed. Sidney Hamilton (far right, back row) was landlord and proprietor of the hotel and also a successful local business man and entrepreneur. He built several streets in the area including Edna Street and Nora Street (named after his daughters) and, of course, Hamilton Street and later helped to create the Goldthorpe Market.

The Goldthorpe Market was established in 1910 under the auspices of Sidney Hamilton. In the background is the shell of the old Hippodrome which caught fire on August 14th 1914. Syd Tierney's memories of Goldthorpe Market, that was held on Market Street, are particularly vivid (*Dearne Local History Group Volume 8*): 'Markets were busy, lively places in the morning, quiet in the afternoons and then came back to life again at nights'. As with most markets it was the oddities that lingered in Syd's memory: The 'quack' doctor that kept many potions and pills and preserved several 'objects' in bottles that had been removed from patients stomachs; the 'Pot Man' who would demonstrate unbreakable crockery by smashing two items together.

Hunters Tea Shop c. 1905.

Meadow Dairy Company Shop Ltd c. 1910. This shop was formerly a Post Office and later became an ice-cream parlour run by the Rossi family.

Members of staff pictured outside the Horse and Groom on Barnsley Road c. 1930s. The Horse and Groom is an old coaching inn and a perfect place to take refreshment on what would have been an arduous ride between Doncaster and Barnsley. It was rebuilt in 1899 and later part of the side section was removed to make way for the beer garden. During these renovations a skeleton was found below the kitchen flagstones.

High Street Goldthorpe decked out in finery for the coronation of 1953.

The bunting was out all over Dearne for the day.

The Recreation Club, Goldthorpe in April 1924. Built in 1910 the club became known as the Reform Club after bankruptcy and later became a Greenfields pub which was recently demolished (1994). At its peak the Club ran successful football and cricket teams.

This early picture is thought to be of the first motor car, a 1904 Royal Beeston Humberette, to travel regularly around the streets of Goldthorpe. It was owned by a Goldthorpe plumber, Harry Gough, who originally came from the West Midlands to set up a business on the Doncaster Road. The car was discovered many years later stored under tarpaulin by his family and sold to a Mexborough garage owner, Mr Harrison, who went on to restore the car to working order.

A charabanc trip for local ladies to celebrate the end of the Second Boer War c. 1902.

A victory parade passes the Horse and Groom on the Doncaster Road to celebrate the end of the war in 1945.

A day trip for the women's section of the Goldthorpe Union Jack Club (Comrades Club) c. 1930. Those identified so far are Kitty Swift, Liz Butterfield, Betty Bretton and Doris Brammer.

Goldthorpe Boys Brigade march up the High Street followed by a small posse of non-members c. 1930.

The last train on the Dearne Valley Railway to stop at Highgate Halt was met by George Walker from Bridal Road (standing left) on 9th September 1951. The line had opened in 1912 and was called the *Titanic* after the liner launched and sunk in that year. Local children also called the service 'pull and push'.

Founder members of the Thurnscoe Harmonic Male Voice Choir. Mr and Mrs Minnikin (seated, centre) were the organising lights behind the choir; Mr Minnikin was the manager of Hickleton Main.

A contrast in dress as the Queen Street and Kelly Street gang line up for this picture. Back row, left to right: T. Gresham, D. Orgill, - ? - , A. Handley, - ? - , - ? - . Middle row: A. Perry, - ? - , B. Cartwright, - ? - , J. Dennis, - ? - , A. Bullars, J. Cartwright, - ? - , - ? - , L. Handley, H. Handley, - ? - . Front row: - ? - , J. Sykes, D. Biggins, - ? - , B. Turner, R. Platts, H. Carter, J. Cooper.

The Salvation Army Band play for Goldthorpe locals on the corner of Headley Street and Barnsley Road c. 1938. On the corner of the street was Burton's radio and electrical shop which stood next to Helliwell's butchers.

Hickleton Main Band at meeting in 1925.

A group of dignitaries and interested onlookers gathered for the opening of the Primitive Methodist Chapel on the Doncaster Road.

A group of Sunday School pupils from the Wesleyan Chapel c. 1928.

Children pose for the camera on the corner of Jackson Street and Railway View in 1939. Those pictured here are Clare Ogden, Alan Cadman, Ron Clarke, Maria Bagshaw, Audrey Griffths, Irene Brayshaw, Joyce Cadman, Jean Bolton, Bob Cook, Mary Gower.

Bored in the back yard, Railway View 1953. Making their own amusement are Eric Hanmer, Lynn Cook, David Lee, David Bannister, Colin Deakin, Linda Knight.

Members of Goldthorpe Home Guard pose for the camera c. 1940. The only identified members of the group are Guy Lewis (seated), the Goldthorpe chemist, and Jack Bulmer (standing left), a deputy at Hickleton Main.

Members of Goldthorpe Civil Defence Group undergo a written examination at the Welfare Hall in 1942.

Goldthorpe Home Guard (E Company, 45th Battalion, Yorkshire) at the back of the Horse and Groom c. 1940. Those identified so far are Irving Randerson, G. Jones, ? Cooper, W. Dyson, Tom Randerson, Fred Taylor, Guy Lewis, Jack Bulmer.

A team photograph of ARP Wardens and Ambulance personnel outside Welfare Hall which was used during the war as an emergency hospital.

Older members of Goldthorpe Working Mens Club on their annual treat in 1936.

Pond Farm on Homecroft Road. The fire station was eventually built on this site; previously the Goldthorpe area had been covered from engines based at the Thurnscoe Station. The name Homecroft was derived from Holmcroft – a local farm field.

A wedding group from December 1949 featuring Jane Johnson, Basil Ward, Ken Knight, Irene Brayshaw, Colin Knight, Albert Brayshaw, Florence Brayshaw, Ann Hudson and Helen Brayshaw.

Goldthorpe Infants in a crowded classroom just before the outbreak of the Second World War. Those identified include Jimmy Morley, Bob Cook, Charlie Randerson.

Goldthorpe Junior Girls School navtivity play in December 1963. The cast featured several budding thespians including: Carol Bullock, Susan Otterwell, Mary Carr, Janet Carham, Christine McGreey, Della Addsetts, Lesley Owen, Andrea Clayton, Hilda Theobald, Gloria Brown, Denice Whalley, Rosemary Clark, Elizabeth Wyatt, Nina Smith, Alison Platts, Ann Wyatt, Allyson Green, Susan Green, Linda Knight, Patricia Horner, Anne Fudge, Joan Marion, Sandra Chapman, Dorothy Coles, Gail Notton.

The 4th Year at Goldthorpe Junior School 1971. Those identified are: Steven Cook, Fred Fox, David Haythorne, Phillip Otterwell, Stephen Bell, Dean Jones, David Rowley, Dean Gratton, Mark Webster, John Kerry, Jayne Cooper, Kathy Hartington, Angela Sindall, Pat Ellis, Karen Latham, Julie Almond, Alison Coulson, Glynis Platten, Sharon White, Elizabeth Anders, David Wharton, Iryna Palancya, Sally Taggart, Deborah Chennel, Cheryl Matthews, Fiona Catterack, Lyn Jones, Christine Hinchcliffe, Debra Crindle. What are they all doing now ?

Goldthorpe Junior School Football Team 1949 featuring Mr Walford, Mr Greenwood, Mr Andrews (teacher), Russell Chambers, Norman Brown, Granville Clegg, Peter Green.

Highgate Junior Mixed School Football team 1957-58.

Goldthorpe Juniors Church team c. 1912. Back row, left to right: William Wild, A. Smith, A. Ward, Tommy Wroth (trainer). Centre row: A. Greenough, - ? -, Arthur Wild, A. Davies, A. Twain. Front row: A Griffiths, Harry Robinson, - ? -.

Goldthorpe United Football Club 1903-04. Back row, left to right: J. Green, W. Hawkins, J. Nightingale, W. Gallimore, W. Carter, T. Baines. Front row: J. Thompson, Stanway, W. Owen, Baker, G. Baines.

Goldthorpe Hotel Darts team c. 1930s. From left to right: Joe Shepherd, - ? - , Angus Hogarth, Harry Formstone, F. Warboys, ? Gardener.

Union Jack Football Club (Comrades) c. 1930. Winners of four local league and cup competitions in a season. Back row, left to right: Baines (secretary), W. Pape, Shepherd, Schofield, Hudson, Speight (goalkeeper), Finney, - ? - , Barker (linesman). Front row: Mellor,

Raynor, Riley, J. Hadlington, Crichley, Wise (trainer). Regular winners of the Sheffield and District League the Comrades team would sometimes get crowds of over a thousand to watch games; at half time packets of aniseed balls and mint humbugs were often distributed.

Goldthorpe Main Street Football Team c. 1930. All the team members were living or had lived on Main Street and were known as the 'Main Street Tigers'. Those identified are Jim Tarmey, Stan Higgs, Thomas Tarmey, Jack Fudge, Eddie Jordan, Eliah Wassell, Eddie Tarmey, Sammy Fudge, Albert Kelly.

Goldthorpe Boys School Football Team, 1931-32 featuring Miles Mitson, Harry Robinson, Malcolm Coman, Ellis Winch, Barry Gillis, Dennis Charlesworth.

36

Goldthorpe Ladies Football Team c. 1939. Back row, left to right: Mr Scothern, Mrs Payne, Mrs Stanton, Mr Lunness, Mrs K. Moorhouse, - ? - , Mrs Bailey, - ? - , Mrs Frost, Mrs Slater. Front row: Mrs Allen, - ? - , Mrs Bullock, Mrs Carter, - ? - , Miss Wortley.

Toward the present day. Ings Lane Football Team c. 1980.

Goldthorpe School sports team that won the Inter School sports trophy in 1938. Back row, left to right: Mr Walford (teacher), Mick Morley, Geoff Waldron, - ? -, - ? -, Lewis Clark, - ? -, Ken Calderbank, Miss Wood. Middle row: - ? -, - ? -, George Roebuck, Rex Lunness, ? Cooper. Front row: Maurice Cooper, Bob Elliot, Jimmy Batty, Billy Hey, Peter Roughly, Walter Cadman.

Hector Calcutt (centre) displays one of the trophys won by the Goldthorpe Table Tennis team c. 1939.

The Reform Club Cricket team and supporters at the Recreation Ground featuring Albert Rowland, Albert Sugden, Ernie Barrett, Roy Bunting, Harry Fereday, George Salisbury, Jack Fudge, George Blunt, Cyril Jackson and Eddie Hall.

The Lindale Dance Band outside Bolton Hall c. 1940. Regular performers were the Marshall twins and 'Juggler' Hollingworth.

Goldthorpe Cycling club at Bawtry c. 1930.

BOXING AT GOLDTHORPE HOTEL.

Boxing at the Goldthorpe Hotel c. 1950. Such tournaments were a regular feature at the Hotel. Those identified so far include Alf Oldfield, Mrs Granger, George Sells, Mrs Young, Jack Young, Jim Tarmey, Bill Scott, Jim Grainger, Denis Oldfield, George Salisbury, Martin Lynsky.

Spectators watching from the cricket pavillion at the Welfare ground have seen many splendid displays with both bat and ball. It was opened by the great Herbert Sutcliffe but due to the actions of a minority it stands today in a state of great disrepair and in urgent need of renovation.

The Highgate Toll Bar c. 1900. This cottage, originally built to collect the tolls on traffic passing along the Doncaster to Barnsley Road, was demolished during the 1920s and was situated near to the present Junior School.

The garden of Bob Weston the undertakers on Cross Street c. 1925. As a contrast to his sombre profession Mr Weston held regular whist drives in his garden as well as entering for the 'best kept garden' competition. He was one of two undertakers in the village during the 1920s: Mr Walker had an undertaking business and his horses and cabs were stabled near the Empire.

Goldthorpe Rugby League team – winners of the cup in the 1924/25 season. The gentleman standing on the far left is believed to David Griffith, later to become the Member of Parliament for Rother Valley.

A Scrivens picture looking down the Barnsley Road c. 1920s. The boy sitting on the wall is George Fischer.

The remnants of what was the fish and chip shop on the corner of Straight Lane and Hope Avenue. The shop was owned and run by the Andrews family who later opened their premises on the Doncaster Road. Many members of the Dearne Local History Group remember collecting a portion of chips here for only 3d.

The High Street in the 1920s. J.R. Hebditch, consultant opticians, is today a lighting and fixtures shop.

Another, more recent view of Goldthorpe Church, taken for a Barnsley exhibition.

Whitworth Street, Goldthorpe c.1950. On the far right at the corner of Queen's Street is Johnstone's shop.

Cycling in the streets of Goldthorpe at the turn of the century.

Two
Bolton-upon-Dearne

All the sights of Bolton-on-Dearne from a postcard of 1920. The official title of the village is 'upon Dearne' but there has been a tendency over the years to use the shortened version.

A view looking toward the old Furlong Road railway bridge on the corner with Bridge Street and The Crescent c. 1945. Irene Dunstan looks over the garden next to the Grocers and Beer Off-Licence which sold fish displayed in crates of ice and large barrels of vinegar which could then be bought by the jug or ladlefull; on the opposite side of the road was situated Mrs Cox's fruit and vegetable shop, now the site of Dr Gopinath's surgery.

The removal and replacement of the old Furlong Road railway bridge in September 1984.

A view down Furlong Road c. 1920. Little has altered in this view; the Crescent is situated to the left and the shop on the right still remains open.

Bolton Common c. 1905. The Common was the original centre of Bolton and would have been surrounded by a cluster of small thatched cottages.

Carr Head Lane, November 1979. These old cottages formed the gateway to the drive to Bolton Hall but were demolished only recently.

The remains of Bolton Hall in September 1976. The hall was built by Doctor Dymond in 1830 and after several owners was purchased by Wath Main for use as a social club. During the Second World War it was comandeered for military use and became Officers quarters; other ranks had to make do with Nissan huts which were erected in the grounds. In 1970 most of the hall was demolished on safety grounds and today the site is occupied by Bolton Residential and Nursing Home. The Local History Group believe this could possibly be one of the hall's outbuildings rather than the main house.

These cottages, on the Wath Road, formed the southern boundary for the estates of Bolton Hall. The tramlines, still visible here, were removed or covered during the 1930s.

Bickerstaffe's Shop on the Mexborough Road seen here in c. 1970, has since been demolished.

On the Mexborough Road c. 1905.

A view down Bolton High Street c. 1905. The old vicarage stands on the left.

The old Post Office at 49, High Street, Bolton: the scene of the murder of Luke White and his wife in December 1856. Luke had established the first post office in Bolton and was popular local grocer and politician. He had had a somewhat wayward past and during his youth he indulged in riotous drinking bouts in Doncaster and was not beyond placing the odd wager. However, he became a respectable member of the Bolton community and his murder (and that of his wife) were never solved. The couple, viciously stabbed many times, were found on the premises by passing locals and the alarm raised. Rumours abounded in the village for many years about the possible perpetrators (including an unfounded suspicion of the local bobby) but perhaps the real answer lay in Luke White's past.

High Street c. 1905.

Hospital Sunday outside the Cross Daggers pub c. 1905. This local gathering would include a procession of those present, dressed in suitable Sunday finery, and numerous side attractions including dancing bears brought from Mexborough. Mr Dickenson, a local builder, is seen standing at the centre of the crowd. The Cross Daggers was demolished and completely rebuilt in 1921.

Angel Street, opposite Bolton Church, April 1957. The building here contained at one time two businesses: Freeman's sweet shop and Barlow's Butchers. The butchers shop was eventually bought out by Mr Barlow's trainee and assistant and was then known as Oldfields. At the back was a small slaughter yard where local school boys could sometimes earn a few extra pennies or even a pork chop when they were recruited to help hold the more persistent lifestock.

A modern view of the Church of St. Andrew at Bolton. The church is one of the oldest in South Yorkshire and is mentioned in the Domesday book. Over the years the weather and, more drastically, subsidence have taken their toll upon the building.

Opposite: Outside the Library at Bolton c. 1910.

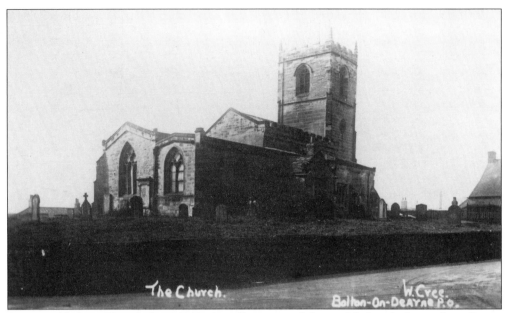

The Church.
W.Cree.
Bolton-On-Dearne P.o.

A view of Bolton Church from 1910. A well positioned, beautiful church dating from Saxon times, although most of the stone work dates from after the Norman invasion. The tower is in sixteenth century perpendicular style while inside Early English arches reside upon Norman pillars and responds. The fourteenth century Lady Chapel is divided from the Chancel by a large arch with the curve less than a meter from floor which probably suggests the original medieval floor remains below. The other notable features of the church include a 'Devil's Door' along the north wall and some of the original Saxon stone encompassed within the north east corner.

Opposite: A Dearne Urban District Council map from October 1938 showing the proposed properties on the Bolton High Street for clearance. The removal of acres of back to back housing may have been economically and politically expedient but it remains easy to be whimsically nostalgic about the communities that were created and fostered by such conditions: row upon row of drying clothes on lines strung from house to house; smiling faces in open doorways; streets without cars. However such notions should always be tempered with a strong dose of reality. John Threkeld in his book *Pits 2* quoted the Medical Officer of Health's report on Bolton: 'Pits are pouring out large volumes of smoke, often two miles in length. You get smoke obscuring the sun and blackening everything'.

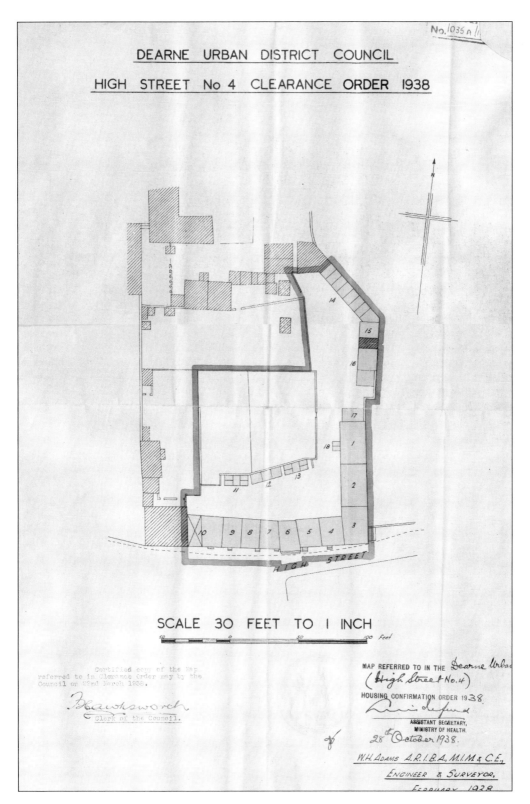

DEARNE URBAN DISTRICT COUNCIL

HIGH STREET No 4 CLEARANCE ORDER 1938

SCALE 30 FEET TO 1 INCH

Houses 45 to 55, High Street, Bolton. A designated clearance area from 1938. The crumbling condition of some of the pre-war housing around the Dearne demonstrated the need for rapid action.

The back view of delapidated Number 45, High Street, just before demolition in 1938.

Houses 1 to 9, New Street, May 1939, pictured here before demolition.

A last conversation on the doorstep No. 5 New Street, Bolton shortly before these houses were swept away.

A group gathers outside a house at the top of Ladycroft c. 1905.

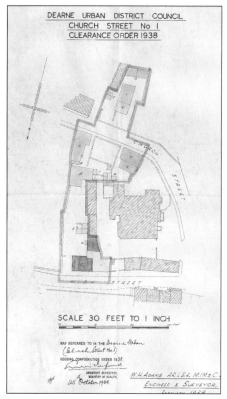

DEARNE URBAN DISTRICT COUNCIL
CHURCH STREET No 1
CLEARANCE ORDER 1938

SCALE 30 FEET TO 1 INCH

A District Council map of the proposed clearance area for Church Street October 1938.

Clearance area number one in Church Street 1938. Over the years Church Street has changed its name: New Street and Pinfold Street being a couple of its *alter egos*. This property was at the top of Church Street near to the junction with the High Street.

Outside No's 42 and 44 on the High Street at Bolton in 1953. The area was declared a clearance area in December of this year but an objection was lodged by the occupants two months later. The order was eventually confirmed and the homes were demolished in 1955.

These terraces (Nos. 11-15) were situated just behind the Church of St Andrew at Bolton, May 1939. On the site today is the bungalow 'Church View' with the public footpath, joining High Street and Church Street, to the side. For over thirty years the Church was encircled by terraced housing.

A rear view of Ladycroft 1954. It was declared a Clearance Area in April 1954 and after objections and a public hearing was eventually demolished.

Ladycroft, just off Station Road, 1954. This street, facing the Junior Girls School, did not survive the demolition programmes of the '50s and '60s. The Post Office which was situated at the top of this street was originally based at the bottom. Looking at the site of neat bungalows and landscaped gardens today it is very difficult to envisage where these terraces stood. The terraces of Ladycroft, full of activity and bustle were among the oldest terraced housing in the area having been built to support the influx of railway workers to Bolton.

The top of Ladycroft in 1905.

N & M Branford builders on Station Road c.1980, a building which today stands empty. Behind this building was situated a slaughter house from which blood regularly flowed onto the road. Station Road was extensively developed during the 1960s and virtually nothing remains of the original housing. To the right of this picture is Bolton Ex-Serviceman's Club.

Station Road c. 1980.

A view toward the junction of Furlong Road and Station Road c. 1910. The Library stands on the site of what is today the Collingwood Hotel. The building to the right housed the Council offices, now belonging to BTCV Enterprises; next door is the small terraced premises from which today the Bolton Tenants and Residents Association is run. The Offices and Library were opened, with suitable civic aplomb, on 30th November 1905.

The Library at Bolton in 1906. The Library, like so many around the country, was built with funds from the Carnegie Trust. Andew Carnegie was the son of a Scottish immigrant weaver who amassed a great fortune through steel businesses in the United States. Such was his philanthropic nature that after he retired in 1901 he devoted much of his wealth to charitable projects.

The old railway bridge on Carr Head Lane c. 1960. Known locally as 'suicide' bridge for the rate at which it claimed victims, it was removed and the whole area landscaped.

The corner of Thurnscoe Road and Wath Road, June 1962. The old village pump was situated just to the side of these houses and was thought to be the site where Bolton's typhoid epidemic began during the 1920s. As new Council Housing was built in Bolton water supplies became irregular as new pipes were laid. Locals began to use the old village pump but the water was infected with the typhoid bacteria. Over 400 people around the area died. Miss Senior of Bolton remembers (*Dearne Past Book 7*): 'In some cases whole families were taken to hospital, the house keys being kept at the council offices until the first member returned home'. To the back of these properties lay the Dearne Light Railway which travelled onto Wath – a service which ended in 1951.

The station at Bolton c. 1920. The station opened after the Midland and North East Railway built the Swinton to Knottingley line in 1879.

On the Wath Road in 1981. Bluff's Farm stands to one side (left) while a new barn now occupies part of the site.

Outside the chapel at Bolton c. 1905. There always seemed to be an endless supply of 'lads' in the streets ready to pose for a photograph.

Dearne Road, Bolton looking back towards the centre of the village c.1915.

Digging through the tip at Ingsfield Lane. Here ground level had finally been reached and the refuse is then ready for burning, September 15th 1950. The Bolton Ings is essentially marsh land that had formed a part of the extensive flood plain of the Dearne over thousands of years and forms an effective natural barrier between Bolton and Wath to the south.

The Bolton bowls team pose with the South Yorkshire Municipal Tournament trophy that they won in 1935.

Whippet training was a passionate hobby and an enjoyable rest from the grind of hard labour for many local folk. The dogs would track a scented trail (usually of aniseed or another potent nose twitcher) to a designated point. Here the dogs are on the verge of release at a training session just off Pickhills Avenue c. 1930.

Priory Road New School c. 1905. The school, just off Station Road, is now known as Lacewood. Hopefully, the children leaning nonchalantly against the wall are not 'skiving' but eagerly awaiting the start of lessons.

An unlicensed gypsy site on the side of Lowfield Road in 1963. The reputation of travellers and gypsies has suffered in recent years especially as the policies of various local councils towards them have and do vary considerably. As the area around the Dearne is controlled by three separate Borough authorities (Barnsley, Rotherham, Doncaster) confusion and controversy over policy is inevitable.

Three
Thurnscoe and Thurnscoe East

The carnival at Thurnscoe in 1911.

TCO.2.   Houghton Road, Thurnscoe.

Houghton Road in Thurnscoe c. 1950 just after the junction with Kingsway. The road here was later narrowed to create parking spaces for shoppers. The shop fronts are mock Elizabethan; Scott's Hardware and China (first left) is today Fenning's DIY; Gregory and Sons is now T.G. Electrical.

Council Houses, Houghton Road, Thurnscoe East

Council Houses on Houghton Road. This postcard has been titled incorrectly as Thurnscoe East. It is, of course, the junction of Houghton Road, Lorne Road and Manor Road taken just after the completion of the new housing estates.

A view up Shepherd Lane toward Thurnscoe Co-operative store c. 1920. The decorative iron railings along each garden were sadly removed soon after this picture was taken. The street (unlike now) is free from traffic and all the properties appear to be still residential.

A view from the corner of the Co-operative store at the junction of Shepherd Lane, Houghton Road and Station Road c. 1910. The Co-op now belongs to the Market Discount Stores.

Station Road junction in 1931. To the left is the entrance to Holly Bush Drive.

Broadway and Schools at Thurnscoe c. 1910.

Farthing Stores at the corner of High Street and Butcher Street c. 1910.

Three Lanes End, Thurnscoe 1890. It is difficult to picture this junction of Shepherd Lane, High Street and Bridge Lane today, such has been the development over the last hundred years.

George Hopkinson's butchers shop at Thurnscoe. George not only successfully wielded a meat cleaver but was a notable speedway rider in the South Yorkshire leagues.

Church of St. Helen, Thurnscoe, was rebuilt in 1887 in early English style on the site of the original Norman church. The tower was constructed in 1729 and within there is a fourteenth century window and an ornately carved eighteenth century wooden font. Sadly, the church, as with many other buildings in the area, has suffered from subsidence.

Parish church, Thurnscoe 1900.

A view of the interior of St Hilda's c. 1910.

In the park at Thurnscoe c. 1920s. The park has suffered in recent years from a combination of weather, vandals and poor resourcing. The ornamental garden is a neglected debris of stone and weed covered with graffiti. The pond is drained and the paths simply used as a shortcut to the shops.

The War Memorial in the park. Unlike many of the decaying facilities within the park the War Memorial remains virtually unchanged since this picture was taken (except for, sadly, the addition of names of those servicemen who gave their lives in the conflicts around the world). A refurbishment in 1995 helped to keep the stonework in good condition. The monument was 'erected by public subscription to the glorious memory and in recognition of the supreme sacrifice made by the persons of this parish'. It reveals the names of 82 servicemen killed in the Great War and 58 in the Second World War. There is also a plaque to Warrant Officer L. Gallagher killed during the Falklands War.

The park at Thurnscoe.

A view from the north to the rear of George Street at Thurnscoe East just before demolition in the late 1950s. Most of the properties in this picture were cleared to make way for the modern development today but a few remain at the entrance to the street at the junction with Lidget Street. The open, grassed area today forms part of the Lidget Lane Industrial Estate. The smoking chimneys and headgears to be seen on the horizon have now gone.

In the scullery of a house on George Street just before demolition in the 1950s.

George Street in 1955.

Part of Church Street in Thurnscoe during demolition in 1968.

The old Almshouses on Rectory Road May 1952. These houses were amongst the oldest in the area having been built in the seventeenth century at the behest of Dr William Spencer, the Rector of Thurnscoe, who wished to provide housing for the poor as a memorial to his wife.

Thurnscoe Hall which stands on the corner of the High Street is today a retirement and nursing home. It was built between 1670 and 1680 by Thomas Shiercliffe and after a succession of owners it was auctioned at the Angel Hotel, Doncaster in 1868 and bought by Thomas Taylor: the Taylor family crest and motto, 'extend fame by deeds', remains above the lodge door today.

Four

Great Houghton

Church of England school rounders team in 1932.

New Street, Great Houghton with Geoff Laycock and Fred Richardson on their milk round in 1947.

Brair's Buildings, Ell's Square 1952.

George White's shop at the end of Edward Street c. 1890.

A view of Houghton Main in the 1970s.

Tables were erected, cakes provided and the bunting draped from house to house for the party at New Street to celebrate the marriage of HRH Margaret on May 6th 1960. The enthusiasm for such events was always greatly aided by the grant of a day off from school or work.

Another party on High Street: this one is to celebrate the Jubilee of King George V in 1935. Local government also caught the party mood – the West Riding County Council gave gift mugs to all infant pupils, propelling pens for junior children and fountain pens for senior pupils. A shilling was also placed in a Yorkshire Penny Bank account for every local child !

The Church School at Great Houghton in 1948.

Houghton Football Club 1931.

Great Houghton St Michael's Football Club, winners of the Junior Cup 1944-45. Back row, left to right: Mr J. Green, Mr Randerson senior, Mr Gomersal, Mr Nicholson, Mr Clubley, Mr Bladen, Mr Randerson junior, Mr Fawcett, Mr Hampson. Top centre: J. W. Harrop, J. Bladen, E. Bladen, W. Shaw, I Pearce, W. Rogers, W. Bladen, F. Leach, W. Stockley. Bottom centre: E. Brinkley (secretary), J. Davis, W. Taylor (Captain), A. Bladen, P.H. Stockley (Asst. secretary). Front row: A. White, W. Robson, S. Ogley, J. Briscoe, J. T. Sykes.

The chapel at Great Houghton, seen here in 1967, was demolished in June 1988.

St. Michael and All Angels Church at Great Houghton. Throughout the centuries the notable and wealthy of England would build themselves a private family chapel – a symbol as much of prestige as a sanctuary for worship. The Rhodes family were no exception and Sir Edward provided the funds and site for this chapel in 1650.

The Co-op at Great Houghton c. 1905 was part of the Barnsley Co-operative Society. Today, especially for a younger generation weaned upon the indoor shopping complex and retail parks, it is difficult to imagine the integral part the Co-op played in the lifes of ordinary folk. In *Dearne Days Remembered* one person recalled that the Co-op 'was at its peak in the 1930s. Every local person had a membership number. The 'divi' [dividend] was given out twice yearly. School children even received classes in how and why the Co-operative Society had been founded'. There were also Co-op stores at Thurnscoe, Bolton and Goldthorpe.

High Street, Great Houghton c. 1960.

A view down Rotherham Road c. 1960.

Lister Row (The Ducky) c. 1900.

Lister Row c. 1905.

The old hall just before demolition c. 1960.

Five
Dearne People

A charity concert at the Highgate club. Those identified include George Tindall, Frank Warboys, Dougie Loudon, Billy Barker, Granville Hill, Fred Pape, Cliff Barker.

Bolton Ladies in Fancy Dress for a charity event during the Great War. Back row, left to right: Mrs Stokes, Mrs Cook, Lily Lunn, Miss Lunn, Muad Watson, May Bunness. Middle row: Martha Thorpe, Mrs Pocklington, Mrs Garbutt. Front: Lena Taylor.

Hickleton Main Prize Band outside Thurnscoe Hall.

Milk delivery girls, Elsie Hanmer and Annie Westwood (nee Robinson), on Frederick Street c. 1930.

The pigeon lofts near the allotments on the bottom of Co-op Street. Pictured here are, left to right: -?-, Harold Brooke, Lawrence 'Al' Brice, 'Fubby' Brice.

Hickleton Main Colliery Ambulence team in 1910. The team were regular winners of the Wood Shield but disbanded in the 1920s. Those identified are, second top left onward, Jack Robinson, Charlie Hanmer, Mr Symester.

Mike Lees (left), the foreign bird judge, with the steward Les Firth, judging the parrot section at Houghton Bird Society Show in 1986. (Courtesy of the *South Yorkshire Times*).

Angela Crosby of Carr Head Lane in Bolton with trophy after she had become British Ladies Featherweight Champion in Tae-Kwon-do in 1986. (Courtesy of the *South Yorkshire Times*).

Bolton Cub Scouts in 1986. Adrian Smith holds the Fitzwilliam Class Trophy won by Bolton Cub Pack for the fifth consecutive year. (Courtesy of the *South Yorkshire Times*).

The survivors of the Barnburgh Mine disaster 1942. In his book *The Day the Earth Trembled* Frank Vernon vividly described the events of April 24 1942 when a tremor caused the floor to rise up in a working shaft: '...the tremor was distinctly felt within a radius of several miles from the pit. Crockery and pans rattled. Loose fittings of all kinds were jolted out of place'. Above the ground the tremor may have caused the breakage of several cups but below the surface the effects were far more damaging: In the Parkgate coal seam, at No. 6 pit, a part of the shaft had risen up trapping eighteen men. Matthew Fairhurst (standing, top right) had been working further away from colleagues and managed to crawl over eighty yards to safety but the other seventeen remained buried. A rescue was rapildy organised involving teams from several pits who had to claw their way through mounds of rock. A human chain was formed to remove the rubble and after 43 hours contact was made with the first group of eight miners. By Monday thirteen men had been rescued but four bodies were removed. As the *South Yorkshire Times* reported that despite their exhaustion the men were in good spirits and one miner, as he was being stretchered away to hospital, was heard to be calculating how much overtime he had earned ! To help with their recuperation the survivors were later sent on a weeks holiday to Blackpool and awarded the Daily Herald Trophy for Industrial Heroism. Other survivors pictured here include Eddie Hall, Bill Fudge, George Mackenzie.

Harold Woodcock from Thurnscoe was a popular local entertainer and magician. Despite his lack of inches he ran a haberdashery stall in Goldthorpe Market although locals remember he had to stand on several boxes in order to pass over change.

Harold's wedding day in Thurnscoe 1950.

Lawrence 'Al' Brice and his band. Al formed this local dance band in the 1930s bringing the latest dance crazes to Dearne. The band, which included Al's three sons, performed regularly at the Astoria attracting people from all over South Yorkshire. On the left are Bill Spencer (drums), Al Brice, Jack Williams (piano); the rest are, back row: Brian Turner, Jack Sutcliffe, Jonty Green, Irvin Brice. Front row: Alec Brice, Roy Brice, Wally Hirst, Ronnie Bond.

With Compliments from

HANMER

PERM. ADDRESS: 205, DONCASTER ROAD, GOLDTHORPE, Nr. ROTHERHAM.

WIRES: HANMER, AMBULANCE, GOLDTHORPE.

Who is here shown fully equipped for Mines Rescue Work. The lamp he uses on these occasions is the "CEAG" Miners' Electric Lamp (Home Office Prize Winner 1912).

Charlie Hanmer – one of Goldthorpe's most famous sons. A miner, photographer and film-maker, Charlie's father had been killed in a pit disaster and this perhaps produced a desire to show the world the hardships that the mining industry demanded. His first film was called the The Toilers but it was his second film Black Diamonds that gained national acclaim, being shown across the country. He is pictured here advertising the Home Office prize winning 'CEAG' electric lamp.

Charlie Hanmer is introduced to the Duke of York at the London premiere of his film *Black Diamonds* on April 13 1932. The venue was the Regal Picture House at Marble Arch with prices for seats varying from 5s to £5. The film was shown in conjunction with the German film *Kameradschaft* which had acquired international acclaim.

Charlie Hanmer and Lord Halifax with members of the *Black Diamonds* cast on the steps of the Goldthorpe Picture House, July 1932. Although the film was greeted with general critical acclaim by the press there were dissenting voices. The *Daily Worker* was not impressed: 'There is, too, about the whole film a nauseating atmosphere of "please-pity-the-poor-miner, he's-almost-human-like-you'.

Local children were hired to help publicise the film: leaflets were handed out and here young 'extras' parade outside the walls of Hickleton Hall with 'Tiny' – the pit pony. Three of 'Tiny's' companions were also given a weeks holiday in honour of the films achievement. There are several copies of *Black Diamonds* still in existence: the Barnsley Archive Service have a video copy but the original nitrate film is stored (in a rarefied atmosphere) in London.

Empire Day at Hickleton Main Cricket Ground, Thurnscoe. The ladies made an appearance in fancy dress representing some of the countries within the Empire, to be followed later by a men's cricket match. Considering the attire of the men in the following picture it is interesting

to remember that the M.C.C. had only recently outlawed the use of a top hat in which to catch the ball. Had the rule change reached the West Riding ?

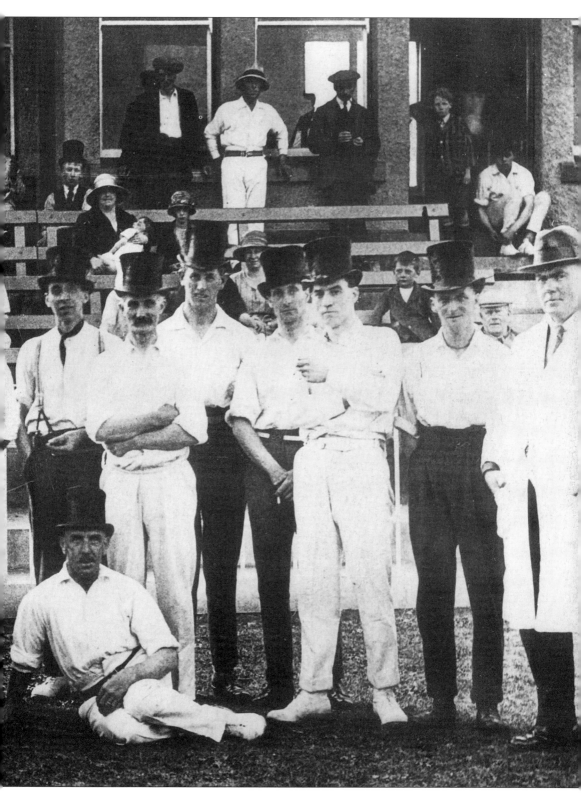

Wilf Copping of Little Houghton, seen here in his England cap, c. 1935. Wilf played for Middlecliffe Rovers and was signed by Leeds United for a £10 signing on fee. Such was his industrious style he was signed by George Allison for the great Arsenal side of the 1930s for £8,500. Nicknamed the 'Iron man' for his uncompromising tackling he was a member of the England team that faced Italy at Highbury in 1934. This was something of a grudge match for Mussolini had publicly declared that each Italian player would receive £150 and a new car if they won. Result: England 3, Italy 2.

Don Walker and Eric Lacey attended Dearneside School in the 1930s and went onto to play for England Schoolboys. Lacey then joined Barnsley and was to finish his career with Wrexham. Many local boys dreamt (and still do) of playing in the professional ranks. Another local, Leslie Thompson of Great Houghton, captained the England Schoolboy side in the 1930s and was regarded by many observers as one of the finest footballing talents of his generation. Tragically he was killed during the Second World War with a potential unfulfilled. His England caps are kept at the Houghton Road School.

Top, left: Eric Lacey, 1937.
Top right: Leslie Thompson played for
Yorkshire Boys and England Schoolboys –
here he is pictured with his cap from 1936.

Ron 'tubby' Latham from Thurnscoe, gold
medal winner at the Lightweight Division at
the Commonwealth Games in New Zealand.

Victor White of Bolton who ran for England in an Athletics meeting against France in 1923.

Hickleton Main Officials outside Thurnscoe Hall. A contrast in dress to the following picture of the Hickleton Deputies. The gentleman sitting far right is Mr J. Dunbar.

Hickleton Main Deputies c. 1905. The first shafts at Hickleton Main were sunk in 1892 and the last coal was brought out in 1988. In his excellent history of the colliery (*The Building And Development of Hickleton Main Colliery 1892-1988*) John Malpass describes the final moments for the pit: 'On Thursday March 31st 1988, the remaining men at Hickleton Main, after the run

down of the pit following the 1984/85 strike, were officially transferred onto the Goldthorpe pit books. The following day the few men who were on the day shift came out of the pit at 12.30 p.m. for a photo session. This marked the end of ninety six years of activity at the pit'.

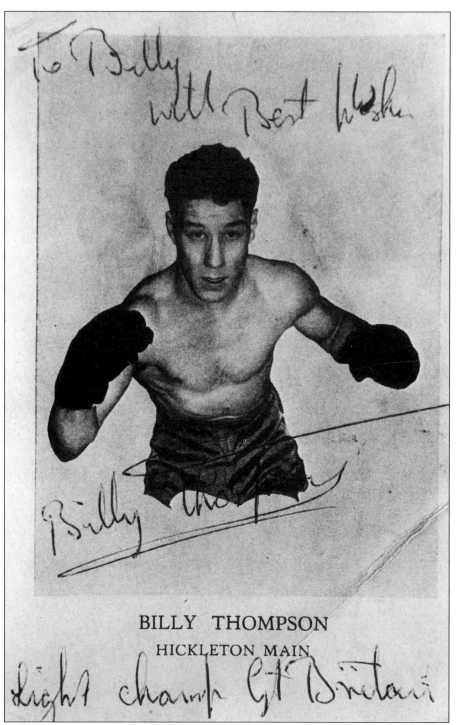

BILLY THOMPSON
HICKLETON MAIN

Billy Thompson, winner of the Lightweight Boxing Championship of Great Britain, in 1948. Thompson, who worked at Hickleton Main, went on to win the European Championship.

John (Jack) Allen – the Hickleton Main Pit policeman c. 1900. He was the last pit bobby to wear uniform at the Colliery. Born at Ullingham near Newmarket he moved to Derbyshire to become an iron furnace worker and later to Goldthorpe and finally to Hickleton Terrace at Thurnscoe.

Fred Reynolds and his son deliver goods on the High Street at Thurnscoe in the 1930s. Reynolds was known locally as 'Staffie' as he originally came from Staffordshire.

Arthur Scargill
and Tony Benn in
deep discussion
during a visit to
Houghton Main
in the 1970s.